PowerKids Readers:

Big Cats™

JAGUARS

Elizabeth Vogel

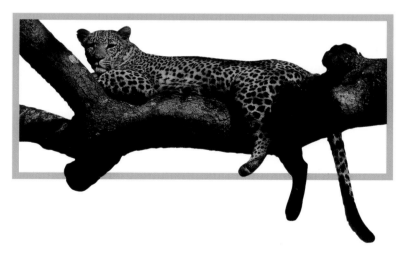

The Rosen Publishing Group's
PowerKids Press™
New York

1

Published in 2002 by The Rosen Publishing Group, Inc.
29 East 21st Street, New York, NY 10010

First Edition

Book design: Michael Donnellan

Photo Credits: p. 5 © Nicolas Russell/The Image Bank; pp. 7, 9 © Gail Shumway/FPG International; p. 11 © Joe Van Os/The Image Bank; pp. 13, 21 © Gerard Lacz/Animals Animals; p. 15 © Partrige OSF/Animals Animals; p. 17 © Digital Vision Ltd.; p. 19 © Richard Kolar/Animals Animals

Vogel, Elizabeth.
Jaguars / Elizabeth Vogel.
   p. cm. — (Big cats)
   ISBN 0–8239–6024–2 (library binding)
   1. Jaguar—Juvenile literature. [1. Jaguar.] I. Title.
   QL737.C23 V634 2002
   599.75'5—dc21

                                                              00–013006

Manufactured in the United States of America

CONTENTS

Jaguars are big cats.
Jaguars like to roar.

Jaguars are the strongest of the big cats.

Jaguars have spots like leopards. Their spots help them hide from other animals.

Jaguars live in
the rain forest.

Jaguars live near water. They like to swim. Jaguars are good swimmers.

Jaguars like to eat meat.
They eat deer, mice,
and turtles.

They find their food at night, but they rest in the daytime.

Jaguars are big, but baby jaguars are small. Baby jaguars are called cubs.

When jaguar cubs are old enough, they learn to hunt from their mother.

WORDS TO KNOW

cubs

deer

rain forest

Here are more books to read about jaguars:

Jaguars
by Don Middleton
Rosen Publishing

Big Cats
by Seymour Simon
Harper Trophy

To learn more about jaguars, check out these Web sites:

http://dialspace.dial.pipex.com/agarman/
    jaguar.htm
www.primenet.com/~brendel/jaguar.html

INDEX

Word Count: 96

Note to Librarians, Teachers, and Parents

PowerKids Readers are specially designed to help emergent and beginning readers build their skills in reading for information. Simple vocabulary and concepts are paired with stunning, detailed images from the natural world around them. Readers will respond to written language by linking meaning with their own everyday experiences and observations. Sentences are short and simple, employing a basic vocabulary of sight words, as well as new words that describe objects or processes that take place in the natural world. Large type, clean design, and photographs corresponding directly to the text all help children to decipher meaning. Features such as a contents page, picture glossary, and index help children to get the most out of PowerKids Readers. They also introduce children to the basic elements of a book, which they will encounter in their future reading experiences. Lists of related books and Web sites encourage kids to explore other sources and to continue the process of learning.